GW00863287

Photoshop for Beginners

Everything You will Need to Know in ONE Book to Master Photoshop like a Pro!

Create Memories that will last a Lifetime with Photoshop Today!

Table of Contents

Introduction

I want to thank you and congratulate you for purchasing the book, *"Photoshop for Beginners: Everything You will Need to Know in ONE Book to Master Photoshop like a Pro!"*

This book contains proven steps and strategies on how to use the basic features of Photoshop in creating memories that will last a lifetime. Photoshop is the universal graphic software used by digital artists, designers, photographers and enthusiasts all over the world. However, it can be quite perplexing to use especially for novice and beginners. There are certain procedures and features that you need to learn by heart in order to fire up the program with ease and get it to run, according to your preference, in no time.

Before you can master Photoshop and be like a pro, you need to learn and familiarize yourself with the various aspects of the program, especially its tools and its various functions. You won't be able to go far with Photoshop if you don't have any idea about its basic features and tools. Although there are various tutorials out there in the internet, it rarely dwells on the basics and is often too complicated for beginners to follow. Moreover, the guides are often spread about, with no clear-cut instructions as to what needs to be tackled first and so on, when you are just beginning to get to know Photoshop.

In this book, you will learn about the most basic features and tools of Photoshop and their fundamental uses in creating beautiful projects that can lend timeless beauty to your memories. Moreover, here in this book, neophyte users can get a good understanding and grasp of the essence of Photoshop. You will be using and employing various tools in Photoshop in accomplishing your creative designs in no time!

Thanks again for downloading this book, I hope you enjoy it!

responsibility of the recipient reader. Under no circumstances will any legal responsibility or blame be held against the publisher for any reparation, damage, or monetary loss due to the information herein, either directly or indirectly.

Respective authors own all copyrights not held by the publisher.

The information herein is offered for informational purposes solely, and is universal as so. The presentation of the information is without contract or any type of guarantee assurance.

The trademarks that are used are without any consent, and the publication of the trademark is without permission or backing by the trademark owner. All trademarks and brands within this book are for clarifying purposes only and are the owned by the owners themselves, not affiliated with this document.

Chapter 1
Getting Started with Photoshop

Photoshop comes with a default workspace and menu. It also comes with the popular Preference, which is infrequently utilized by users. This area actually has various functions. It lets you adapt the application based on your specific style of designing. It also supports you in using existing computer attributes to enhance the general operation of the program.

File Handling Preference

You can actually simplify the process of saving by adjusting the File Handling Preferences. You can even alter the way your cursor appears. For instance, you can make your paintbrush look like a paintbrush or just a crosshair, whenever you paint. You can make some other changes to the program, depending on what you like by altering your preference on your file handling.

Why change the preference of Photoshop in accordance to your desire? Well, if you are uncomfortable with the way menus and palettes are presented in Photoshop, it can affect your productivity, creativity and your speed when doing the job. The more comfortable you are with your current settings, the faster and more efficient you will be in accomplishing your work in Photoshop.

At this point, you may not be able to appreciate the use of units and rulers in Photoshop. As you delve deeper into the program, however, you will realize that when you work on pictures or images, accuracy is paramount. It goes the same for guides, grids and slices. You may not take this preference seriously but when you are confronted with having to work on a blue-sea picture set against a blue guide, you will definitely realize what I am talking about.

At this point, it is important to know that the Scratch Disk, RAM and Image Cache that you can find in your Preference menu can actually increase the speed of your Photoshop processes by up to 20%.

Boosting Photoshop performance

One of the most formidable graphic applications ever built, Photoshop, as such, needs immense computing power to run. This is especially true when it comes to working on big documents. If your Photoshop application is inadequately optimized, it will need longer have enough time to process files. When you are trying to beat a deadline, this will definitely be a setback. On the lighter side of things, however, you should know that the application can be configured to operate efficiently. Hence, to boost the performance of Photoshop, you just point to Edit, then to Preferences and click on Performance. By clicking on Performance, a dialog box, which contains numerous options to configure the program to run more efficiently, will pop up.

Scratch Disk

No, we are not referring to the one that disc jockeys utilize to produce that scratchy sound. Scratch Disk actually refers to the free space accessible in any drive, which Photoshop utilizes when there is inadequate RAM to perform a process. Photoshop actually needs 5x the size of an active file in adjoining hard drive area.

For instance, if you are working on a 150MB file, you will require 750MB space of adjoining hard drive. Otherwise, an error message will display that you have an out of space Scratch Disk. It will work to your advantage if you can use supplementary hard drives to give the application the capacity to split the load of processing, thus enhancing performance. You can see all existing internal disks in the dialog box of Preferences. To achieve optimal performance, it is advisable to tangibly connect a Scratch Disc to your computer.

Stay away from detachable media such as USBs and Enclosures, networks and even rewritable VCDs. It is highly recommended to utilize a 4 or 6 pin wire drives since this can give at least 20% increase in speed when employed as a Scratch Disk. Moreover, it will also redound to prime performance when you utilize a Scratch Disk other than the drive used as virtual memory.

RAM and History States

In Photoshop, you can actually make up to 1,000 undo. The History States is the area, which controls the quantity of undo. Nevertheless, you have to realize that when you increase History States, the RAM that Photoshop utilizes in managing the history pane also increases. This means that when you assign more RAM to manage the history pane, lesser memory will be allocated to perform other tasks in Photoshop, which can result to a reduced performance. Freeing up RAM by decreasing the quantity of History states will make Photoshop work faster and more efficiently.

In reality, the more Random Access Memory (RAM) you can allocate to Photoshop, the more proficient it will perform, specifically in opening huge files. Know that whenever you augment components to a file, its working size will increase accordingly. The working size of a particular file determines the size of the RAM used and not the file's open size.

General Preferences

To modify other aspects of your Photoshop project, you can find other diverse selections in the General setting under the Preferences of the Edit menu. For instance, if you want your open documents to auto-update or be able to use the Shift key to switch tools and emit a sound whenever a particular procedure is finished, you can just turn these features on or off in the Options menu. Another thing, which you can adjust in the General preference, is the size of a picture during a Place. This is useful in relocating a copied picture to the clipboard of the operating system or employing the animated zoom, which allows for an incessant zooming in and out of your file.

Other General Preferences options are the following:

- ***Zoom clicked Point to Center***, which allows you to zoom in on the midpoint of a specific clicked area.

- ***Enable Flick Panning***, which allows for the rapid movement of the mouse over the picture instead of pressing down on the mouse.

- ***Snap vector Tools and Transforms to Pixel Grid***, which allows the cracking of vector tools and changes to the grid of the pixel.

- ***Dynamic Color Sliders,*** which allows you to preview the effects of color just within the slider.

File Handling Preferences

The Photoshop program makes it possible for you to save documents using diverse formats such as BMP, TIFF, JEPG or EPS. If you want to change the data saved in a document, you just browse over the File Handling Preference dialog box to choose the desired changes. Depending on what you desire, you can set the operation to save in the background (allows you to work while still saving) based on time interval.

In case the program suddenly crashes, it will automatically try to salvage the file and open it. To avoid increasing the size of your file, preview of the image is characteristically small. Once you have already saved your document, you can do anything with it, including changing it by using other applications designed to edit images. The selection in the File compatibility allows you to utilize or save a document that will be modified in Photoshop or migrated to other programs.

File Handling Options

To make use of the various options in File Handling, click on File Handling under the Preferences of Edit menu. You can then choose the File saving selections you want to utilize, such as:

Image previews – You can choose from the following options: Ask when saving, Never Save or Always Save.

Save in background – allows you to save files automatically behind the scene, while you continue working.

Save as to original folder – lets you save the document to its original folder.

Chapter 2
Working in Photoshop

Photoshop workspace

The first thing that will be shown to you when you click on the Photoshop icon or program is your workspace. Upon opening the program, a default workspace will be displayed. In the default workspace, you will see the following:

- *Menu bar* – The Photoshop menu bar is more or less similar with the menu bars of other programs. You can see this bar at the top of your workspace window and it comprises diverse menu options for the program's tools.

- *Toolbox* – In your default workspace, your toolbox is located running down at the left of your window. It encompasses Photoshop tools' shortcuts.

- *Options bar* – It is located right under the menu bar and includes options (depending on the context you choose) for various tools. It also covers the workspace menu, where you put in palette arrangements and save projects.

- **_Document windows_** – Every time you open a document, it will have its own document window wherein you can see the particular graphics you have loaded. It has its own status bar along its bottom, which sits at the right side of the zoom percentage display pertaining to the specific document at hand.

- **_Palettes_** – The document you opened, which is displayed on your document window, is also shown on an individual pane or more popularly known as palette. It is located at the right hand side of your document window.

If you don't like the default workspace that comes with the program, you can always customize it according to your preference.

Making a Modified User Interface

There are actually hundreds of options available in Photoshop menus. You can't see them all at once, since majority of them are hidden in pull-down menus or dialog boxes. Thus, if you are intimidated with all the options, Photoshop gives you the option to create your own user Interface to suit your preference and style. You can always delete your customized interface anytime you no longer want such and restore the default Photoshop interface.

Working with a Modified User Interface

Open the Window menu, click on Workspace and point to keyboard shortcuts & Menus. Hit the Menu, point to create a New Set button, key in a name for the new button and point to save. You should then click the arrow for the Set list, then choose a listing of customized User Interfaces. You can choose the Delete Set (to erase a set) or the Restore Original Set (to choose the default set). Click on the Menu for list arrow, point to Panel Menus or Application menus for the elements you want to change.

Expand the menu that includes the command you want to change by clicking the arrow. To display or hide a command, click on the icon of visibility that is linked to it. To alter the color of the button command, hit on the arrow for Color list and choose a particular color for the chosen command. Lastly, hit on the Save All Changes (to save the new customized interface) and then OK.

Modifying your workspace

There are various ways to customize your workspace to suit you or your project's needs. The most important thing to remember is that nearly all within your workspace can be rearranged or repositioned. You can customize your workspace by doing the following:

Altering the appearance of the menu bar

You can virtually add color to the stuff in your menu bar and control what specific items should appear on the bar. To accomplish this, just go to the menu under the Edit bar and utilize the dialog box to change the palette menus and the menu bar itself. The program comes with a set of its own shortcuts to commands in the menu. You can change these shortcuts according to your preference if you want to. However, it is well recommended to assign your own shortcuts only when you have fully mastered using the default ones to avoid confusion.

Changing the looks of your Toolbox

You will find that you can practically move the toolbox anywhere you want to in your screen by just clicking on the light gray portion at its top and dragging it to your preferred location. You can also choose from various layouts of the toolbox by clicking on the double arrow, which you can find on top.

A different looking Options bar

If you prefer to have a new location for your options bar instead of its usual place, you can do so by just clicking on its handle, which is located on the left side and then move it to your preferred area. You will find that when you move the handle of your Options bar, either near the top or bottom of the screen, it will 'anchor' itself automatically.

Configuring palettes

There are various methods of configuring your palettes. For instance, if you want to make the dock bigger or smaller, you just click on the double arrows located near the top of its dock. Should you want to detach a specific palette from its palette group and move it to another group, all you have to do is to drag the palette tab from its original cluster towards the new one. You can also pull out some of your palette tables out of their dock and close the others. If you want to display a closed palette again, you just go to the Window and choose the palette you want to display or show.

Establishing Cursor Preferences

Photoshop corresponds to us through the use of visual prompts; the most conspicuous one is in the form of a cursor. For instance, if the cursor displays like the letter I, this signifies that it is time to key in text. When the cursor takes the form of an hourglass, it is saving a file or when it looks like a magnifying glass, you can click on an image with it and it will automatically transform the size of the view. To give you better management over how the application communicates with you, just head on to the Cursor Preferences and select the options to your liking.

Document windows status bar

By default, the status bar will only display the size of the document file. You will see the file size as two numbers separated by a forward slash with the first number indicating the estimate file size of the images (all layers are merged) and the second number as the estimate of the total size of the file (with all layers intact). You can actually set the status bar to display other information like version number of the file or its dimension in pixel. To accomplish this, you just need to click on the icon of an arrow, which you can find next to the status bar, choose Show then select the information you want to display.

Saving your customized workspace

After repositioning and configuring the panels in your workspace based on your preference, go to your Options bar and click the workspace menu. You can also click on the window menu and then point to workspace. Type a name for your workspace, choose check boxes to save Menus or keyboard shortcuts then click Save.

Deleting a customized workspace

If you don't like the customized workspace you have created and saved anymore, you can delete it by clicking on your Options bar and choosing workspace Menu. Click on the arrow or the workspace list and click on the workspace filename you want to delete. Bear in mind that you cannot delete a workspace you are currently using. You must first switch to another workspace or the default one first before you can delete by clicking the delete button and the "yes" button to confirm the action.

Now that you know about Photoshop workspace, customizing it and the general location of things, it's time to try your hands working in Photoshop.

The first thing that you need to do if you are going to make a particular project is to create a new document.

Creating a new document

To create a new file, select New in the File menu bar. Doing so will display a different dialog frame. You can change the settings and appearance of the document according to your preference by choosing the appropriate button on the menu bar.

Opening files

If you already have a saved document, you can choose "Open" in the File menu bar. You can actually open several files all at once by keeping the Ctrl button down and clicking on the documents you wish to open in the dialog box.

Saving files

To save a Photoshop file you have created, click on the Save on the File menu. This action will save your file in the format of a Photoshop Document for newly created files.

Web-friendly formats

Know that Photoshop files cannot be inserted into a page in the web on their own. You need to export them first and save them into formats that the web can read such as PNGs, JPEGs and GIFs.

GIF - This format has a maximum number of 256 colors. It also backs up animation and transparency. It can function best with files that have a large area of the same color.

> *Colors* – If you want to lessen the number of colors used in an image in GIF format, you just adjust the color settings.

> *Dither amount* – This refers to a compression method wherein the dots pattern is diverse to lend an illusion of a gradient in color. By altering the dither, there will be a more perceptible dilapidation for images with a huge number of colors merged together.

> *Matte color* - If you are working on a non-transparent image, using matte colors will outline the background color of the image. For transparent images, on the other hand, the matte color will help in the blending of

the edges of your image into the background of the page.

PNG

Just like the GIF format, PNG works well with solid-color images and supports transparency. However, it is considered as a much better format to GIF since it also supports transparency for colored areas. PNG formats produce better quality image at a smaller size than GIF.

JPEG

If your image or images have beyond 256 colors and gradients, you will do well working with JPEG. Files saved in JPEG formats are flattened. This means that with this type of format, information regarding the image is actually lost, which causes the reduction in its quality.

Quality – If you change the number in the Quality box, the compression level of the image will be altered. If you reduce the quality, it will result into pixilation or a blurry image. On the other hand, if you set it too high, it will result into a very large file, which takes a lot of time to download. Thus, to avoid the extreme, you need to slowly adjust the quality to the point where the image is still acceptable but not too large for easy downloading.

Chapter 3
Photoshop Layers

One of the most formidable attributes of Photoshop, which lets you work on one area of an image without disrupting the rest, is the Photoshop Layers. For beginners, the idea of using layers can be quite daunting. However, once you get the feel of it, you will wonder how you have gotten through using Photoshop without them.

Through the translucent parts of any layer, the layers underneath that layer will show through. Just click on the matching eye icon in the Palette of Layers if you want to display and hide each layer in the image.

Each layer cluster is denoted by a folder icon. By hitting the triangle image, which is located at the left part of the folder icon, you can either expand or collapse the layer groups. Shell layer clusters inside each one of them by just dragging a specific folder emblem into another. To systematize your layers, you can categorize them into layer groups by clicking on Layer>point to New and then >Group. By the way, each group of layer displays similarly as any uncategorized layers on the Palette for Layers.

To help you work with Photoshop effectively and efficiently by using Layers, here are some important things to learn and understand.

- **Renaming layers** – Just double-click on the layer name.

- **Alter the transparency of a layer** – Modify its opacity by utilizing the Opacity slider or you can also type a value in the Opacity box. You can see the box when you selected the Crop, Move or Selections tools.

- **Duplicating a layer** –There are two options for duplicating a chosen layer. You can just press Control (CTRL) J command or drag the layer while pressing the Alt option key at the same time.

- **Select multiple layers** – Hold the CTRL key while clicking on the layer names. This action will form a temporary link between the selected layers, which permits you to delete, move them all, etc. as one.

- **Link layers together** – You can do this by holding down the CTRL or SHIFT command while clicking on the layers.

After choosing all the layers you wish to link, click the button (Link layers) at the left section of the bottom part of the Layers Palette (indicated by a chain icon). Unlike selecting multiple layers, linking allows the link relationship to stay even after you have chosen a different layer.

- **Unlinking layers** – Just choose one of the layers in the link and then go to Layer, click on Unlink Layers. For single layer unlinking, just choose the layer you like to remove from the linkage and click on its matching link icon. If you only want to temporarily unlink a layer, hold down the Shift key and click on its link icon. The temporary unlinking will be indicated by a red letter "X", which will appear over the icon of the link. You can reactivate the link by holding the Shift key again and clicking on the link icon.

- **Rearranging layers** – You can accomplish this by just dragging the layer either below or above the rest of the layers.

- **Using shortcut to select a layer** – Press on ALT key. This will allow you to move up and down through the layers in the Palette for Layers.

- **Creating a New layer** – Just press Shift-Control-N keys. This will display the dialog box for a New Layer. If you want a shortcut, just press on Shift-Control-Alt-N keys.

Chapter 4
Using the Photoshop Toolbox

Looking at the structure of the toolbox of the Photoshop, one may get a little intimidated and confused with all the icons in it and what it is all for. The toolbox is divided into four major classifications for easy maneuvering.

The classification of the tools is the following:

- Selection, slice and crop tools

- Retouch and Paint Tools

- Drawing and Type Tools

- Annotations and measurements tools.

The toolbox also includes the Foreground and Background colors.

We will not be discussing every detail of all the functions of the tools since it will definitely take us more than just 6 chapters if we go into all the details. Nevertheless, we will discuss all the vital tools and their most fundamental functions to allow you to have a full grasp of the beauty of Photoshop and utilize it like a professional artist.

Comprised of the Marquee, Move, Lasso and Magic wand tools, these are the most basic gizmo that you will use when selecting an image for your project.

- **Marquee tools** – These are utilized for choosing objects with square, ellipse and rectangle shapes.

- **Move Tool** – It is characterized by an arrow and a cross-like with arrow points and is used to move layers, objects and selections.

- **Lasso tools** – It comprises several tools such as the magnetic lasso tool and polygonal lasso tool that are used to make asymmetrical objects.

- **Crop tool** – This tool will allow you to cut, clip or trim an active image without actually resizing it. Using this tool will be just like as if you are using a scissor to cut out a desired portion of the image.

- **Magic wand tool** – It allows you to choose an area of the same colors in a single click such as the blue in a painting depicting the sky.

- **Eraser tool** – As the name implies, this tool is used to obliterate parts of a layer, selection or image.

- **Retouch tools** – Otherwise called as healing tools, these will actually help the user mend the defects in the image, such as red eye and blemishes.

- **Clone tools** – With the help of this tool, you can actually duplicate an image precisely. You can use this tool by choosing a starting point anywhere on the original image then drawing elsewhere utilizing that starting point as base, thereby cloning the image source.

- **Fill tools** – You can use this tool to fill up areas, layers and selections with gradient or solid colors in one click.

- **Sharpen, blur and smudge tools** – The first two tools are used to specifically define and blur the edges of an image, while the smudge tool is used to smear an image utilizing finger-paint.

- **Painting tools** – If you want to draw strokes in graphics, you can utilize the brush and pencil tools for the painting job. You can modify these tools according to your needs to achieve that picture-perfect drawing.

- **Dodge Burn and Sponge tools** – If you want to lighten some parts of an image, you can use dodge tool while you use the Burn if you want to darken the image. You can use the Sponge tool to deluge or un-deluge areas of an image.

- **Foreground and background color** – You utilize these tools to paint, fill objects or shapes, color text and achieve a lot more things with Photoshop. These tools conveniently allow you to see what colors are currently being selected and switch between two diverse colors with ease.

- **Pen tools** – You can use these tools when you want to make clear paths and shapes that can you can then utilize as vector objects. You can scale these types of objects to any size you like.

- **Type tools** – Utilize these tools when you want to create and set type in vertical or horizontal direction, in a specific image.

- **Custom shapes tools** – These are vector objects that can be automatically made out of the list of presets.

How to use these tools?

Depending on your needs, you don't actually need to use all the tools in one particular project. Nevertheless, whenever you want to use a tool from the Toolbox, all you have to do is to click on 'drawing' or 'icon' once. Bear in mind that if a particular tool displayed shows a black arrow in the right corner of its bottom, it indicates that there are still more tools belonging to such category hidden beneath it.

To choose one of the hidden tools, just hold down the mouse button over the display of hidden tools and release the mouse once you get to the one you would like to utilize.

Chapter 5
Type Tool for Beginners

Photoshop is not your usual application for typesetting by definition. However, it has some dominant type attributes. For instance, it lets you produce PostScript text directly to your printer with a PostScript selection. Through this feature, you don't have to put Photoshop figures into applications dedicated for typesetting just to make some lines of writing. Furthermore, the menu for Type in Photoshop allows you to see fonts as they are in display or print. This feature is actually a time saver, especially for users who utilize various fonts. To aid you in choosing the font and type options, you can take advantage of the preferences in the Type menu.

Considered by many as one of the most powerful and expedient tools of Photoshop, Type Tool has a lot of potentials that a lot of users are not familiar yet. However, considering that this book is intended for new users who want to use Photoshop like a pro, let us start with the most basic features of this tool.

Fundamentals

The tool that you should utilize if you want to make mathematical forms and vector figures to express the representations of a script is the Type. It is represented by little T in the Tool Bar. If you want its shortcut, just type the letter (T). You will find that it offers four options when you hover the click over the T tool or hold Shift plus the T key for quite a few times. It will display the options Vertical Type Mask, Horizontal Type Mask, Vertical Type and Horizontal Type.

Vertical Type Mask tool, Horizontal Type Mask Tool – These tools let you make a Quick mask using the Type form as a Selection.

- **Vertical Type** – It allows the Type tool to make vertical text from the topmost down and from right to left. This tool is valuable if you want to experiment with typographic project and in writing languages like Chinese or Japanese.

- **Horizontal Type Tool** – This will allow the tool to make horizontal typical text, which is left to right and top to bottom.

You will observe that once you have chosen your preferred Type Tool, the cursor of the mouse transforms into the usual letter I Type cursor.

This signifies that the file you are currently working on is now prepared for text to be placed on it.

Working with Type Selection

First, you click the menu then point to Preference and Type. You can then choose the Type selections you want to utilize as indicated below, before clicking OK.

- **Show font names in English** – Click on this if you want to show non-classical fonts, displaying their English equivalent.

- **Enable Missing Glyph Protection** – You can select this option to automatically choose erroneous, indecipherable characters between classical and non-classical fonts.

- **Use smart quotes** – Choose this if you want to utilize a pair of quotation marks.

- **Choose text engine options** – You can click on this if you want to show middle Easter or East Asian types.

It is important to note that a 72-point font size will output in print as a 1-inch tall type. With this knowledge, you can determine how large the fonts will show when produced into print.

Make Type Layer

You can make text layer in two ways, Paragraph and Point Type.

Paragraph- – This method will make Text layer with text wrapping into a bounding box. This option is quite useful for web and print design. To put in a Paragraph layer, you must make a bounding box first. Just click and drag the cursor slantwise until you achieve your preferred size.

Point - This selection will make Type layer into a solo line. Put the break lines by clicking "Enter" or "Return". To make a Point type layer, select your preferred Type Tool (Vertical or Horizontal Text), then click just with your cursor anywhere you like to place the text. Start to input the text, then just click on either the Enter key or the Command + Enter.

Chapter 6
Working with Photoshop Shortcuts

To say that Photoshop is a time-consuming application is definitely not an overstatement. Using it will use a great deal of your time. This is the main reason why the application utilizes shortcut keys. According to several studies conducted, using shortcut keys in Photoshop will allow you to save one hour for every 8 hours you spent on the program.

In the normal flow of the process, if you want to open a new file in Photoshop, you point to file then click on New. For a faster and direct approach, however, you can just hit Ctrl plus the letter N to accomplish the same goal. When you opt for shortcut keys, lessen the utilization of the mouse, which hastens the process. What's significant about Photoshop shortcut keys is that they don't only come in hundreds, but also give you the freedom to create your very own shortcuts!

How can you define your own shortcut key? First, click the Edit in the menu and point to keyboard shortcuts. Hit on the arrow in the left column to enable the expansion of the menu that includes the command where you can make your own shortcut. Choose the desired item from the list of commands then utilize the keyboard to make your new shortcut. Lastly, click on Accept then OK.

Other things you can do with shortcuts

As much as Photoshop allows you to create your own shortcut, you can also choose to delete any or all of them if you want. Furthermore, you can also make a printout of the shortcut keys predefined by Photoshop, which you can make as your manual reference. Use the shortcuts in your panel tools in your toolbox menu and Application menus. To accomplish the task, you wish to do, just click Edit in the File menu, point to keyboard shortcuts and just click on the appropriate button you wish to employ such as Add, Delete or Summarize shortcuts.

Chapter 7
Working with Measuring Units and Guides

Rulers and Measuring Units

For beginners, it is important to have some basic understanding of the concept of units and rulers in Photoshop. Although the rules and measuring units of info do not impact the quality of your work per se, these will actually aid in the evaluation of information in a file coherent with the particular output tool.

You can determine the exact height and width of an active file with the use of the rule units. You can utilize the column size dimensions in providing you with pertinent information that the program needs to make files with columns like in brochures, magazines and newspapers.

Working with rules and units' options:

- Click on the Units & Rulers under the Preferences in the Edit menu.

- Choose the Units you want to employ:

- ○ *Type* – Select this if you are working with millimeters, points or pixels.

- ○ *Rulers* – This will place a pre-defined computing method for the Ruler Bar. For instance, it will be noteworthy to remember that outputs in printers are usually measured in inches while those displayed in monitors are by pixel.

- Choose the settings for column dimension you want to utilize:

  - ○ *Gutter* – This is the space between the columns

- Choose the Preset resolution settings for your new document.

  - ○ *Print resolution* – lets you modify the resolution of the print and value of measurement for default setting of printing.

  - ○ *Screen resolution* – lets you modify the resolution of the print and value of measurement for default display on the screen.

- Hit on the PostScript or the traditional selection gauging systems for the type tool for Photoshop. Click OK.

Guides, Grid and Slices Selection

Guides and grid are also as important as precision when you are working with images. If you don't know how to use the grid and guides, you will find that you will encounter some confusion when you get to edit an image, which has a similar color with your guide, thus, you need to maneuver your way through these options to optimize your work.

Do you know that you can actually alter a vertical guide into a horizontal guide, and vice versa? Just point to the Ruler Bar and pull a guide into your active document window. However, before releasing mouse, press down the ALT key. This action will switch the direction automatically.

- To work with Guides, Grid and slices option, you must go to Edit menu, click on Preferences and then point to Guides, Grid and Slices. At this point, you can choose the Guides you want to employ, such as:

- *Style* – Choose a pre-defined line or dashed line for showing guidelines.

- *Color* – Choose a pre-defined color for showing guides.

- Get to choose the Smart Guides selection you want to employ (color guide).

• Choose the Grid selection you want to utilize:

- *Style* – Choose a pre-defined color for showing grids.

- *Color* – Choose a pre-defined style of dots, dashed lines or lines for showing grids.

- *Gridline Every* – allows you to enter a value for the frequency of times a grid line will show within a specific document.

- *Subdivisions* – allows you to enter a value for the number of times that a subdivision line will show between every gridline.

- Choose the Slices selections you want to employ:

  o *Line color* – choose a pre-defined line color for showing file slices.

  o *Show Slice Numbers* – Choose the check box to show a number for every slice in the upper left area of the slice.

It is important to remember that when you choose a line color, opt for a color other than the guide line and grid colors. You can discern the grids and guides for user-made lines this way. You can select color selection for Guides, Grid and Slices if you are not contented with the pre-defined colors in the menus. To change the color selection, go to the color boxes that are located on the right area of the Preferences dialog box and just choose any color from the Color Picker.

Plug-Ins Preferences

In Photoshop, a plug-in means a peripheral code modal that broadens the functionality of an application. This graphic application comes with numerous pre-installed Plug-In like Filter Gallery and Camera Raw. However, users also have the freedom to install other third-party plug-ins. If you need to install third party Plug-

In, ensure that you get to save it to pre-defined Plug-In folder of Photoshop. This is to ensure their availability in the Photoshop application. Should you want to adjust something in Plug-Ins, go to Plug-Ins Preferences and specify your selection.

For extension panels, you can choose whether to permit extensions to link to the Internet and load the panels for utilization on Window Menu's Extension submenu. Regarding Filters, you can indicate whether you like to display all Filter Gallery clusters and their name on the Filter menu or not.

If you are not familiar with a particular installed Plug-In, you can learn something about it by pointing to Help and clicking on Plug-Ins. Just choose the Plug-in you want to know about to help you learn something about it.

Conclusion

Thank you again for purchasing this book!

I hope this book was able to help you to start a new project in Photoshop and navigate through its numerous menus and commands.

The next step is to master all what you have learned in this book in preparation for a more advanced undertaking in Photoshop.

Finally, if you enjoyed this book, then I'd like to ask you for a favor, would you be kind enough to leave a review for this book on Amazon? It'd be greatly appreciated!

Thank you and good luck!

20728037R00027

Printed in Poland
by Amazon Fulfillment
Poland Sp. z o.o., Wrocław